An Album of
the Great Depression

An Album of
the Great Depression

by William Loren Katz

FRANKLIN WATTS | NEW YORK | LONDON | 1978

Cover design by Ginger Giles

Photographs courtesy of:
National Archives: p. 8 (bottom); NA/U.S. War
Department General Staff: p. 8 (top); NA/Civilian
Conservation Corps: p. 51 (top right); NA/Office of
War Information: p. 72 (bottom); William Loren
Katz Collection: pp. 8 (center), 84 (right); New
York Times: p. 11 (center); Library of Congress:
pp. 11 (top and bottom), 13, 15 (top and bottom),
16, 17, 18, 21 (top right), 22 (all), 23, 27, 28, 30
(all), 32, 33, 37 (bottom right), 39 (top and bottom),
40 (top), 42, 44 (top and center), 46 (left and right),
47, 48 (top), 52 (left and right), 54, 55, 56, 57, 58,
59, 60, 61, 62 (all), 64, 65 (top and bottom), 66
(left and right), 67 (left and right), 68 (top and bottom), 69, 70 (all), 72 (top left and right, center left
and right), 74, 75, 76 (left and right), 77 (all), 79
(left and right), 80 (top and center left and right),
81, 83 (all), 84 (left), 85 (all), 86 (left and right),
87 (left and right), 88 (all), 90 (left and right), 91,
92 (top and center left and right); Farm Security
Administration: pp. 12, 19, 21 (top left and bottom),
25, 29, 34, 37 (top and bottom left), 40 (bottom),
43, 44 (bottom), 45, 48 (bottom left and right), 53,
92 (bottom); National Relief Administration: p. 38;
Wide World Photos: p. 26; Civilian Conservation
Corps: p. 51 (left and bottom); Pathé News: p. 71;
Paramount Pictures, Inc.: p. 80 (bottom). *Cover photographs courtesy of:* Farm Security Administration.

Library of Congress Cataloging in Publication Data

Katz, William Loren.
    An album of the Great Depression.

    Bibliography: p.
    Includes index.
    SUMMARY: Discusses the causes, events, and ef-
fects of the Great Depression and highlights the programs designed to alleviate it.
    1. Depressions—1929—United States—Juvenile lit-
erature. [1. Depressions—1929]   I. Title.
HB3717 1929.K35   330.9'73'0916   77-21413
ISBN 0-531-02914-X

Contents

For Jane and Dave

Introduction:
A Personal Recollection

My memory of the Great Depression is of a child living on West 13th Street, New York City, and attending P.S. 41 Manhattan. My life was not touched by its tragedies, for my family had some money and enough to eat. True, my father's business went from bad to worse and finally bankrupt and my mother had to take a job. My father hated being jobless and my mother hated her job as a social worker investigating who deserved relief.

My father had no interest in politics until he attended a La Guardia rally. Galvanized into action, he helped organize unions and fought for racial equality. There were stimulating current events discussions at our dinner table, and interesting black and white visitors. I recall being taken to a Madison Square Garden rally protesting against Hitler's threat to Czechoslovakia.

I remember one birthday when I received only three comic books and a bag of cherries. But my life on 13th Street was very happy—we kids played marbles in the gutter (few cars then), flipped Indian and war cards, listened to ball games, "The Shadow," and "The Green Hornet" on the radio, and played punchball. On Saturdays we spent a dime to see cowboy movies and sometimes a nickel for a hot dog (with free root beer) on 14th Street. The Police Athletic League opened a field on our corner and sometimes took us to baseball games at Yankee Stadium or the Polo Grounds.

I knew others fared far worse than my family. Standing on the lunch line at P.S. 41 one day I heard a girl talking about her birthday present: a dime. My black friends across the street, Harry and Emily, visited the Salvation Army each Friday and returned with enough free groceries to last their family a week. Harry rarely had enough money to go to the movies with us.

We were bored by school, thrilled to athletics, dug swing music, feared Hitler and war and admired President Roosevelt. My cousin Mimi and I posed for a WPA mural painted by Rockwell Kent. It was an exciting time to grow up.

William Loren Katz

(7)

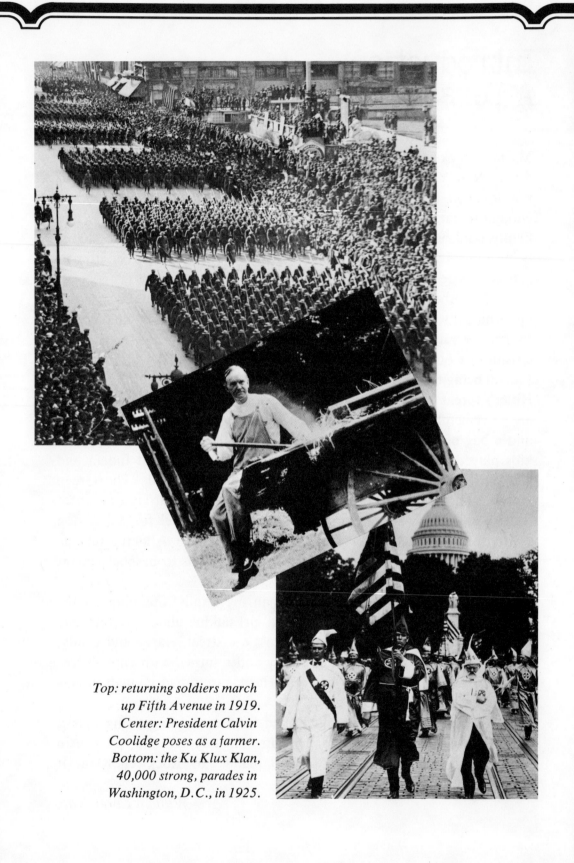

Top: returning soldiers march up Fifth Avenue in 1919. Center: President Calvin Coolidge poses as a farmer. Bottom: the Ku Klux Klan, 40,000 strong, parades in Washington, D.C., in 1925.

Prologue:
America in the Twenties

AMERICA TURNS ISOLATIONIST

Huge parades celebrated the return of American troops from Europe after World War I. But as the cheering faded and the 1920s began, bitterness grew in the land. The United States had fought "to make the world safe for democracy" in a "war to end all wars." But it was soon clear democracy and peace had not won.

A new crop of dictators ruled in Germany, Italy, Japan, and Russia. Despite the new League of Nations, dictators began planning another, bigger world war.

In disgust, America turned its back on Europe. The U.S. Congress refused to join the League of Nations. It cut back immigration. Intolerance grew inside America, too. The Ku Klux Klan, claiming more than 4,000,000 members, rode again. These night riders lashed out at blacks, Jews, Catholics, foreigners, union members, and radicals.

PROSPERITY AND POVERTY

The 1920s was also an age of business expansion. More people than ever before owned houses, radios, cars, and telephones. The American President, Calvin Coolidge, proudly announced, "The business of America is business" and "The man who builds a factory, builds a temple. The man who works there, worships there."

Not everyone shared in this prosperity. While increasing their productivity by 40 percent, workers' wages rose only 7 percent. The average yearly wage for a fifty-hour week was $1,500. Minorities and women received even less, and children less still. Throughout the 1920s farmers were in a depression, their prices falling lower and lower.

This was the Jazz Age. But behind the blaring jazz bands and dancing couples loomed the tragic figure of economic crisis. As the twenties drew to a close, that figure began to move toward the middle of the stage.

The Big Crash of 1929

THE STOCK MARKET

In 1928 the Republican Presidential candidate, Herbert Hoover, won the election. He predicted a day "when poverty will be banished from this nation."

Part of his confidence was based on the rising stock market. By 1929, prices of shares had been rising steadily. More than 1,500,000 people owned shares in companies. Not just the rich, but housewives, elevator operators, newsboys, and sales clerks bought and sold corporation stocks. No one seemed to lose.

Most bought shares "on margin." This meant they put down only a tenth of the value. When prices rose and they sold their stock at a profit, everything was fine. But what if prices began to fall and they *had* to sell? No one worried about that. On September 3, 1929, stocks reached an all-time high and everyone was jubilant.

THE CRASH

Slowly that October stocks began to slide down in price. On October 24, 1929—later called "Black Thursday"—stock prices plummeted. When "on margin" buyers could not come up with more money, their stocks had to be sold for a loss. Brokers on the stock exchange shouted for buyers. Now there were no answers.

Bankers rushed to buy stocks, to issue calming statements. Then on October 29, 1929, there was a "Black Tuesday" to match the "Black Thursday." Some 16,000,000 shares were sold at a loss, one stock diving from $100 to $3.

Businessmen, bankers, and President Hoover again and again announced that business was sound, the panic was temporary, prosperity was just around the corner. They were whistling in the dark.

(10)

Top: one of many anti-gloom demonstrations, citizens of St. Augustine, Florida, meet to bury "J. Fuller Gloom" so good times can return. Center: the New York Times *headlines "Black Thursday." Notice how business leaders and the* Times *tried to bury the bad news with optimism. Bottom: President Herbert Hoover. Throughout the hard times he announced that "prosperity is just around the corner" and rejected demands to provide relief.*

TWO CENTS In Greater New York | THREE CENTS Within 200 Miles | FOUR CENTS Elsewhere Except 7th and 8th Postal Zone

OCTOBER 25, 1929.

WORST STOCK CRASH STEMMED BY BANKS;
12,894,650-SHARE DAY SWAMPS MARKET;
LEADERS CONFER, FIND CONDITIONS SOUND

FINANCIERS EASE TENSION

Five Wall Street Bankers Hold Two Meetings at Morgan Office.

BREAK 'TECHNICAL'

Wall Street Optimistic After Stormy Day; Clerical Work May Force Holiday Tomorrow

Confidence in the soundness of the stock market structure, notwithstanding the upheaval of the last few days, was voiced last night by bankers and other financial institutions and by the heads of some of the industrial executives as expressed by Wall Street ended the day general that the selling had got in an optimistic feeling that the selling had got apparent weakness in the market alarmed over the steady liquidation their private wires these brokers against further thoughtless selling of the National City Bank, de-

LOSSES RECOVERED IN PA

Upward Trend With 200,0
Order

TICKE

Going from Bad to Worse

THE ECONOMY UNRAVELS

The stock market crash upset the entire economy. With fewer investments, factories and mines fired workers. Some factories even closed down. The unemployed had no income to spend on food, clothing, or shelter. More stores and factories had to close. Now even more people were jobless and had no funds to purchase goods or pay bills. Each step down led to more disasters.

People lined up at banks to remove their savings. But banks had also lost money in the stock market. Banks began to close. People soon had no money to pay their rent, buy groceries, or dress their children.

Wages fell by 15 percent, but employed people felt lucky to keep their jobs. Bread still sold for 7 cents a loaf and butter for 49 cents a pound. But people bought less bread and butter.

(13)

Opposite: standing on a San Francisco breadline. Above: the Great Depression was worldwide. Police in London arrest women protesting unemployment.

LOCAL RELIEF

To aid those without money to buy food, cities set up soup kitchens and breadlines. The hungry lined up for a crust of bread, a small cup of thin, tasteless, lukewarm soup. People looked down, hoping their friends would not notice them.

Some towns soon ran out of relief funds, out of bread and soup. Salt Lake City reported scores of citizens starving, children unable to attend school as they had no clothes to wear. A Pennsylvania man wrote:

> *This is the first time in my life that I have asked for help, but the way things are now I must. I have been out of work for a long time and my wife is sick in bed and needs medicine, and no money to buy nothing to eat and what is a fellow going to do. I don't want to steal but I won't let my wife and boy cry for something to eat.*

For the first time many Americans heard the cry of hungry children, both next door and at home.

HOOVERVILLES

Within six months of the stock market crash 4,000,000 persons had lost jobs. Their clothes began to look ragged and some had to move out of their homes. Yet President Hoover issued promises that the hard times would soon be over.

From Seattle to New York a new sight dotted urban landscapes. The homeless constructed living quarters out of cardboard and wooden boxes, newspapers, tin, and parts of old cars. In these "Hoovervilles" the jobless walked around aimlessly, their pockets turned inside out as "Hoover flags."

Unemployment Councils formed in cities, with Communists among the leaders. In March 1930 more than 10,000 jobless men and women fought with police in New York City's Union Square. Communists had called the demonstration, but many more than Communists had come out.

(14)

Top: the Seattle, Washington, Hooverville stood at the entrance to the city. Bottom: this Chicago Hooverville housed six men calling themselves "the Lost Battalion." The news caption accompanying the photograph said "How they exist no one knows."

THE APPLE SELLER

A new figure appeared on city streets. He was a veteran of World War I, out of work, and he sold apples for 5 cents apiece. For $2.25 he bought a box of seventy-two apples, spent 10 cents on bags and 10 cents on carfare.

Then he stood for hours hoping to sell all his apples. If he sold all of them, he made a profit of $1.15 for his family.

President Hoover said, "Many people have left their jobs for the more profitable one of selling apples." Living and eating well in the White House, he did not understand the desperation of others.

Opposite: this apple seller, father of two, was jobless for sixteen months. Above: in the summer of 1931 President Hoover was photographed on the White House lawn with troops from Fort Meyer. He would soon order them back to the capital to defend himself from the unemployed.

The Terrible Year of 1932

A NATIONAL CALAMITY

By 1932 more than 14,000,000 Americans were jobless, one-third of the work force. The number may have been as high as 20,000,000 jobless, no one is sure. Many others worked only part time. Some 5,000 banks failed, leaving millions without their savings. Stocks had fallen to 11 percent of their 1929 prices. Investors lost $75,000,000,000, more than three times the cost of the war for America.

(18)

Above: on Chicago's South State Street gangster Al Capone established this soup kitchen to feed the starving. Opposite: the grim, shocked face of the disinherited.

Factories and stores were closed and men and women milled around. Some searched for food in garbage cans and others gathered on street corners to talk of revolution. No one knew what had happened to their country, their lives. It was as though an invisible enemy had defeated the United States, and stood astride the land.

URBAN TROUBLE

In some cities people invaded food markets to seize milk, bread, and canned goods for their families. Chicago had 600,000 unemployed and New York City had 1,000,000. In Chicago about 200 women slept in Grant and Lincoln parks—without shelter or protection. People talked of "a dictator to set America right again."

Young people left home for the open road. Children dropped out of school because they had no clothes to wear. Some were admitted to hospitals suffering from malnutrition.

RURAL AGONY

Catastrophe struck agriculture as well. It cost more to produce crops and livestock than their selling price. To drive up prices, farmers dumped milk into ditches, burned wheat and corn, and slaughtered pigs and cattle. With guns, they prevented others from bringing food to market. Some piled their vegetables, meat, and milk on trucks and handed them out to those starving in cities.

Without profits, farmers could not pay their bank mortgages. Banks foreclosed on farms and 273,000 families lost their homes in 1932. Farm people loaded their belongings and children into old, battered cars and trucks and headed west. By 1940 the population of Oregon, Washington, and California had grown by 1,000,000.

Some had no cars, no way to move their families. In the South white and black men and women picked cotton for $1 a day, and sometimes got cheated out of that. In Harlan County, Kentucky, an unemployed coal miner wrote, "We have been eating . . . such weeds as cows eat."

(20)

Top, left: this woman, with her child and their belongings, joined thousands of others on the road. Top, right: rather than sell at low prices, farmers dumped their milk on highways. Bottom: a ghost town left by the Depression in Hale County, Alabama.

The Depression as a Personal Tragedy

COLLAPSE OF TRADITIONS

The hard times shattered many beliefs. Farmers, once proud of feeding the nation, cut back food production to raise prices. Heads of families, proud of their ability to care for their families, had to turn to charity or government for aid. The jobless father felt ashamed in front of his friends, wife, and family. Each family had its own personal nightmare.

Opposite, top: a young man tries to uphold middle-class ways despite poverty. Opposite, left: for one job in a Brooklyn, New York, cemetery in 1932, these men all applied. Opposite, right: hunger marchers reach the nation's capital in late 1931. Above: veterans hoping for government loans receive Red Cross coffee.

(23)

Family quarrels were more frequent, bitter, and disastrous. Some families fell apart. Children crying from hunger depressed mothers, fathers, brothers, and sisters. Many left home. Elderly people rarely found work and felt they were a special burden.

In a nation that prided itself on its industriousness, there was not enough work. The more creative were more frustrated.

PERSONAL COMBAT WITH HARD TIMES

In Philadelphia a storekeeper told of one large family: "Eleven children in that house. They've got no shoes, no pants. In the house no chairs. My God, you go in there, you cry, that's all." He did more than cry. He supplied them with groceries on credit.

In other cities police and teachers bought lunches for hungry students. In Hoovervilles and migrant camps people shared food and warmth with strangers. Families pitched in, sharing the little there was to eat and wear.

THE AMERICAN DREAM SHATTERS

Sometimes people lost more than they could stand. A woman in Newburgh, New York, drowned her four-year-old son, saying, "I couldn't feed him, and I couldn't see him go hungry." During a veterans' parade hungry children invaded the lunch laid out for the marchers and devoured it. As hope faded, the birthrate dropped and suicides rose.

Middle-class men tried to hide their hurt and loss in lies. Some dressed as though going to work each day. Once in town they changed into old clothes and sold apples or begged. "I haven't had a steady job in more than two years," said one New Yorker. "Sometimes I feel like a murderer. What's wrong with me, that I can't protect my children."

Some 350 Americans a day applied for resettlement in Soviet Russia. When Amtorg, a Soviet trade agency, advertised for 6,000 skilled Americans to work in Russia, 100,000 applied. Good people wept in frustration or turned to crime to feed their families.

A mother with two infants faces the hard times.

Marching on Washington in 1932

THE BONUS EXPEDITIONARY FORCE (BEF)

Congress had been talking of passing a bonus bill for veterans of the World War. But now millions were starving and veterans flocked to Washington carrying signs reading "Heroes in 1917—Bums in 1932." By May 15,000 to 20,000 veterans and their families camped in the Capital.

They set up old Army tents or built Hoovervilles out of scrap metal, wood, and cardboard. They drilled, sang old Army songs, and staged an orderly parade up Pennsylvania Avenue. Then they waited for Congress to pass the bonus bill. They waited in vain.

PRESIDENT HOOVER REACTS

The President became alarmed at so many hungry people in the Capital. He refused to meet with the BEF leaders and called them Communists. Police guarded the White House day and night. A block away, on all sides, barricades went up and traffic was halted. The White House prepared for attack.

On a humid, hot July day, the 28th, police ordered the veterans to leave their encampments. A brick hit a police officer, who later died. The police opened fire. A veteran fell dead. Rioting broke out.

Opposite: bonus marchers battle police, July 7, 1932. Above: demonstrators before Congress ask for unemployment insurance.

(27)

President Hoover ordered General Douglas MacArthur, Chief of Staff, to call out federal troops. MacArthur personally led the assault, assisted by Major Dwight D. Eisenhower. Major George Patton brought up the mounted soldiers. Six tanks accompanied the assault on the veterans' tents and families.

VETERANS DISPERSED

Tear gas hung in the air and blood ran in Washington. Troops with drawn swords marched on ragged men, women, and children. Two babies died because of tear gas. President Hoover and General MacArthur called the attack successful and claimed they had halted a Red take-over of the government.

Bewildered families stumbled home. They came seeking a bonus for fighting for America, and federal troops had fired on, tear-gased, and driven them from their nation's Capital.

RELIEF DEMONSTRATION MARCH

In December 1932 another ragged band of 3,000 shuffled into Washington seeking relief. To protect the city 9,000 police were called out and U.S. troops stood by.

Vice President Charles Curtis met their delegation with "You just hand me your petition. You needn't make any speech. I have only a few minutes' time."

Nothing in America's past or in President Hoover's personal beliefs could convince him that his administration should help the destitute. Relief was a community responsibility; if government stepped in, the obligations of citizens would stop. Hoover held firm to his belief in community action to aid the distressed and starving—even when it did not work.

(29)

Opposite: bonus marchers camp out in the shadow of the Capitol. Above: a hunger marcher in late 1932 is fed in the Capitol.

The Election of 1932

HOOVER VERSUS ROOSEVELT

The Republicans, calling themselves "the party of prosperity," nominated Herbert Hoover to stand for reelection. The Democrats nominated Franklin D. Roosevelt, governor of New York, and newspaper reporters took his initials and called him FDR.

Crippled by polio as a young man, FDR always needed steel supports to get to his feet. But voters were quickly diverted from his handicap by his engaging smile and his warm, vibrant voice. When he addressed radio audiences as "my friends," and promised "a new deal" for "the forgotten man," they listened.

THE CAMPAIGN

Hoover stood on his record and his belief that government must not take over relief from communities. In 1929 few disagreed with him, but this was 1932 and millions were unemployed. Hoover was blamed for the Great Depression, and his attitude was called callous. Hoover called FDR "an innovator," but voters wanted an innovator.

President Hoover faced audiences that applauded his mention of FDR. Citizens came down to pelt Hoover's campaign train with eggs and tomatoes. FDR's own promises were vague, offering only some experiments to pull the country out of the hard times.

FDR LANDSLIDE

On election day FDR carried forty-two states and Hoover only six. That night FDR admitted to his son, "I'm just afraid I may not have the strength to do this job." Many shared that fear.

In Miami, Florida, a month before he took office, FDR rode in a motorcade with his friend Mayor Anton Cermak of Chicago. Suddenly Joe Zangara, a deranged bricklayer, fired wildly at Roosevelt. Mayor Cermak fell fatally wounded by the pistol shots, but FDR was unhurt. Americans were heartened by FDR's courage under fire.

(31)

Top: to keep up appearances, President Hoover attended a baseball game as election time approached. Center: hunger stalked the land at election time, as seen in this soup line. Bottom: the Democratic Presidential nominees, Roosevelt and Garner, campaigning with their wives.

Inauguration of a President, 1933

A STRANGE CEREMONY

In Washington Inauguration Day looked more like a preparation for an invasion. General MacArthur had placed Army machine gunners at strategic points along the parade. Troops stood by. FDR and Hoover rode along, hardly talking to each other.

Everyone stopped work to hear the new President's words. FDR's voice was calm, reassuring, confident:

Let me first assert my firm belief that the only thing we have to fear is fear itself—nameless, unreasoning, unjustified terror which paralyzes needed efforts to convert retreat into advance.

He asked for broad powers to deal with the crisis—"as great as the power that would be given to me if we were in fact invaded by a foreign foe."

FDR told his fellow citizens, "The people of the United States have not failed." He said Americans wanted "direct, vigorous action. They have asked for discipline and direction under leadership." Almost half a million people wrote FDR letters approving the speech and pledging their support.

THE NEW DEAL TAKES SHAPE

That night the President did not attend the Inaugural Ball. Instead, he and his advisers burned the lights late at the White House. On his first Monday FDR announced he was closing the nation's banks until they could reopen on a sound basis. Depositors had been lining up to collect $41,000,000,000 when banks had only $6,000,000,000 on hand.

*Opposite: President Hoover and President-elect
Roosevelt prepare to ride from the White
House to the Inauguration, and both managed
to smile. Above: Frances Perkins, Secretary of
Labor, and General Hugh Johnson, head of
the National Recovery Administration.*

FDR appointed some liberal people to his Cabinet. Frances Perkins, as Secretary of Labor, became the first woman Cabinet member. Henry Wallace, an Iowa farmer, Republican, and scientist, became the Secretary of Agriculture. Harold Ickes, a Progressive, became Secretary of the Interior.

The President also had his special friends and advisers, his "Brain Trust." They included college professors and philosophers who had little experience in government but many ideas. Above all, FDR wanted to be open to new ways of solving the Depression.

THE NEW DEAL GOAL

Roosevelt's aim was to rescue the country from economic collapse. He meant to prove capitalism and free enterprise could work. He sought to improve business and the profit system, not eliminate them. Yet his enemies would accuse him of driving toward socialism.

A week after he took office, FDR addressed the nation in a "fireside chat." In simple, clear tones, like a teacher, he explained the steps his administration was going to take. People loved his fireside chats, for they seemed to mean he was taking them into his confidence.

He announced he would ask Congress to repeal Prohibition. Liquor would flow again legally. FDR's theme song had been "Happy Days Are Here Again." Now, said the drinkers, it would be a reality.

In 1933, restaurant prices
on the Bowery reflected the
state of the economy FDR faced.

The First "Hundred Days"

THE NEW PRESIDENT ACTS

FDR once said that if he were not a good President, he would be the last President. In the first hundred days of his administration, he and his advisers moved swiftly. FDR met with his Cabinet twice a week, gave ten speeches, sent fifteen messages to Congress, guided fourteen major laws to passage, gave many press conferences, and created the Good Neighbor foreign policy.

President Hoover had warned the country that FDR was an innovator. He was right. "Take a method and try it," FDR said. "If it fails, try another. But above all, try something." That was his New Deal.

THE "HUNDRED DAYS" LEGISLATION

In the period from March 9 to June 16, 1933, the following New Deal laws were passed:

Banks were put under strict federal control to protect depositors · 500,000,000 federal dollars were provided for the destitute · Federal control was imposed on the stock market to protect investors · The Civilian Conservation Corps (CCC) gave forestry jobs to the young · The Agricultural Adjustment Act (AAA) sought to help farmers gain high prices · Federal credit was extended to homeowners to meet mortgages · The Tennessee Valley Authority (TVA) built dams and offered cheap electricity to that vast southern region · The National Recovery Administration (NRA) sought to stimulate business and unions.

A NEW BONUS MARCH

Halfway through the hundred days a new Bonus Army shuffled into Washington. This time the President housed them at an Army camp, provided them with meals, and had Army doctors take care of their sick. A Navy band played for them.

The leaders were welcomed at the White House. No police or troops tried to drive them off. Instead, Eleanor Roosevelt came to visit. Said one veteran, "Hoover sent the Army, Roosevelt sent his wife."

(36)

Top: the desperation of the times is seen in this bleak picture of Bethlehem, Pennsylvania. Bottom, left: a migrant worker in Michigan sleeps in a barn. Bottom, right: a minister in New York has to sell apples.

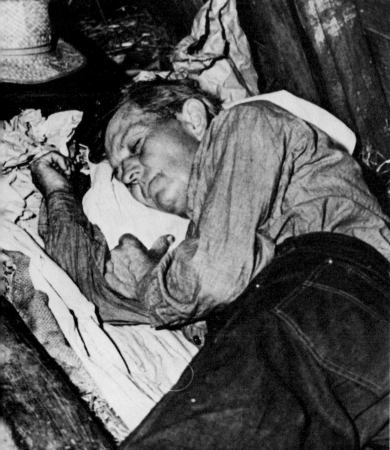

NRA and General Hugh Johnson

GETTING BUSINESS MOVING AGAIN

While the New Deal fed people with relief, it aimed to get them back to work, earning their own way. The NRA, run by tough, ex-General Hugh Johnson, asked corporations to set their own work codes, hire people, and begin producing again.

To speed recovery, Johnson launched advertising campaigns, mass meetings, and huge parades. Companies that cooperated displayed the NRA "Blue Eagle" flag and the NRA slogan "We Do Our Part."

(38)

Slowly business began to pick up. The hard times were far from over, but despair had begun to fade. After a while, companies lost interest in the NRA, and its campaign collapsed.

NRA BOOST TO UNIONS

If the Depression was to end, wages had to rise. If unions were strong, they would demand higher wages for their members. Part 7a of the NRA law guaranteed unions the right to bargain for their members.

During the twenties unions had been too weak to defeat their employers, to win higher wages. Employers had been aided by the government. But now this was changing. The Norris-La Guardia Act kept the government from breaking strikes and halting picketing and boycotts with injunctions.

With the Norris-La Guardia Act and provision 7a of the NRA law, unions began to grow in strength. But the march of workers infuriated some businessmen. They began to blame FDR for "communizing everything decent in America."

Opposite: the NRA began with emblems and fanfare, but fizzled after a short time. Above: these enthusiastic union members had no union when the New Deal began in 1933. But by 1940, when this picture was taken, they were in Local 600 of the United Auto Workers, and supported the President, who had aided their cause. Right: Senator George Norris, cosponsor of the Norris-La Guardia Labor Act, was one of many Americans to point the finger of guilt at Wall Street during the hard times.

New Deal Aid to Farmers

AGRICULTURAL COLLAPSE

By the time FDR entered the White House a million farmers had lost their land. Banks foreclosed and sent tractors out to level their homes. Grim families piled into jalopies and rode west.

But some remained to demonstrate. At foreclosure auctions a homestead was bought by a friend for a penny and returned. No one dared bid higher, and sheriffs were helpless. Farmers organized to prevent the sale of produce. On Route 20, Iowa farmers sang:

> *Let's call a farmers' holiday*
> *A holiday let's hold.*
> *We'll eat our wheat and ham and eggs*
> *And let them eat their gold.*

"For a farmer to buy a toothbrush," said John A. Simpson, president of the National Farmers' Union, "he would have to sell eight dozen eggs and he then would owe two cents. A farmer must sell forty pounds of cotton to buy a good shirt." The more the farmer produced and carried to market, the lower prices fell.

FDR PLANS

New Deal aid to farmers took many forms. The AAA paid farmers to plant fewer crops, use less land. This was designed to drive up prices by making shortages.

The Farm Loan Administration supplied credit for farmers. The CCC hired thousands of young people to protect the environment. From Canada to Texas, these young people planted a shelter-belt of 200,000,000 trees a thousand miles across the continent and a hundred miles deep.

Secretary of Agriculture Henry A. Wallace provided information on growing crops, preventing erosion, and preserving the land.

Top: Iowa farmers, seeking to prevent foreclosures,
compelled officials to sign no more mortgage foreclosures.
In this photograph they are also compelling a deputy
sheriff to kiss the American flag. Bottom: FDR made
personal visits, usually at election time, to rural areas.

THE TENNESSEE VALLEY AUTHORITY

The TVA was designed to aid residents of a poverty-stricken, often flooded land. It built twenty dams in ten years to manufacture inexpensive electricity. Thousands of people found work; roads and schools for the region were constructed. Malnutrition, joblessness, and ignorance were things of the past.

But TVA also introduced what many felt was a dangerous idea to the United States. TVA was the first time government had gone into business. The federal government operated the dams, sold the electricity, hired the workers. Denounced then as socialistic, a danger to free enterprise, TVA lives on and so does private enterprise.

Above: government aid for agriculture included group discussions for those living in migratory camps, such as this one in Florida. Opposite: the TVA did more than build dams, but flood control was its initial aim.

Top: FDR turned to southern problems, such as cotton production. An FSA supervisor confers with a Louisiana farmer. Center: Georgia farmers signing up to receive government loans. Bottom: the plight of elderly people and the very young concerned the Second New Deal.

The Second "Hundred Days"

RISING NEW DEAL POWER

The New Deal faced its first popularity test in the congressional elections of 1934. The Democrats gained 20 seats in the House and in the Senate, and now controlled forty-one of forty-eight governorships. This was an impressive vote of approval by the American people.

FDR and his "Brain Trust" renewed their attack on the Depression. This time they focused on the plight of the small farmers and workers, for they also sought to gain votes from these groups.

THE SECOND "HUNDRED DAYS" LAWS

To deal with the hard times, the Second New Deal passed these laws:

Began the Works Progress Administration (WPA) to create jobs · Shifted relief for the destitute back to the states · The Resettlement Administration provided homes for urban and rural families driven from their homes, or gave loans for new homes · For the young, old, and dependent, Social Security became a reality · The National Labor Relations Act (NLRA) set up special elections in plants to determine the employees' choice of unions · The National Youth Administration (NYA) helped young people find jobs · A new FDR law increased taxes on the wealthy and corporations.

FDR with two of his key advisors, Rexford G. Tugwell (left), who headed the Farm Security Administration, and Will Alexander (right), who headed the National Youth Administratoin.

Putting America to Work

HARRY HOPKINS AND THE WPA

Private industry recovered so slowly that social worker Harry Hopkins convinced FDR that the federal government must hire people. Only by putting people to work, even for the government, Hopkins argued, would relief become unnecessary.

Hopkins was put in charge of the WPA plan to build schools, hospitals, airports, playgrounds, and highways. Some 8,500,000 were hired for 1,410,000 different projects. The WPA built or improved approximately 2,500 hospitals, 5,900 schools, 1,000 airports, 13,000 playgrounds, 124,000 bridges, 125,000 public buildings, and 8,200 parks.

Critics complained that WPA employees did not work but leaned on their shovels all day. "Do you work?" went a joke of the day. "No, I'm on the WPA," came the answer.

AID TO THE CREATIVE

The WPA did more than put shovels in workers' hands and construct buildings. It offered jobs to the creative in a host of fields. It hired musicians, historians, dancers, actors, cartoonists, writers, and artists.

The WPA provided free or inexpensive puppet shows, dance recitals, musical presentations, and dramas. It hired playwrights, directors, scene designers, actors, make-up artists, and orchestras—people who would have remained on breadlines. These men and women developed a vibrant, experimental dramatic form.

WPA plays appeared in English, Spanish, Yiddish, and French. Sinclair Lewis's *It Can't Happen Here,* a drama of a fascist capture of America, appeared simultaneously on twenty-one stages in eighteen cities. WPA murals, painted by unemployed noted artists, appeared in schools, post offices, and libraries.

Opposite, left: Harry Hopkins was put in charge of the controversial WPA. Opposite, right: a park built by WPA labor is dedicated by New York City's Mayor La Guardia. Above: some 2,000 marchers before the White House to demand more WPA projects and jobs.

(47)

Social Security Is Born in America

THE TOWNSEND PLAN

One day Dr. Francis Townsend looked out his medical office window and saw three old women picking through the garbage. Shocked, he decided government must aid the elderly. He proposed a monthly federal pension of first $150, and then $200 for each person sixty or older.

His plan caught fire. Townsend clubs formed from coast to coast. The *Townsend National Weekly* sold 200,000 copies. Though his plan was impractical, politicans feared to criticize it.

FDR did not criticize it, but borrowed parts to make his own Social Security plan.

THE SOCIAL SECURITY ACT OF 1935

FDR's plan was based on payroll taxes, paid by people until they were sixty-five and became eligible for the pension. He justified the idea in these words: "With those taxes in there, no damn politician can ever scrap my social security program." The law provided a pension of $10 to $85 a month, and made the money available to widows or surviving children of the recipient.

The new law also aided states in taking care of the blind, deaf, physically or mentally handicapped, homeless, and dependent or delinquent children. With these federal funds states could establish worthwhile arrangements.

A final part of the new plan was state-federal unemployment insurance to cover those temporarily out of work.

Until Social Security came into existence, growing old or being handicapped was an even more painful experience in America than it is today. Social Security helped change that.

Top: domestic servants were also excluded from Social Security benefits. Bottom, left: agricultural workers, such as this couple, were not included among those to receive Social Security benefits. Bottom, right: this unemployed Illinois mine worker was entitled to unemployment insurance under Social Security.

(49)

Emphasis on the Young

JOBLESSNESS AND THE YOUNG

A Pennsylvania girl, age nine, wrote to her governor:

> *There are nine of us in the family. My father is out of work for a couple of months and we haven't got a thing to eat in the house. . . . I go to school each day. My other sister hain't got any shoes or clothes to wear to go to school. My mother goes in her bare feet and she crys every night that we don't have the help.*

In Chicago a government committee discovered this scene at the city dump: when a garbage truck pulled up to unload, thirty-five men, women, and children began digging through the garbage with sticks and hands to find food.

It was a difficult time for the young. Finding jobs was next to impossible, gathering on street corners was easy, and stealing was tempting. Threatening young people with jail was useless. "That's what we want," said one. "That will give us food and a place to sleep."

YOUTH ON THE MOVE

A million or more restless young people, black and white, male and female, left home and school for the open road in the early years of the Depression.

They were called "Depression Nomads" and climbed aboard freight trains heading east, west, north, and south. In 1932 the Southern Pacific Railroad reported its guards threw off 683,000 people from their freight trains. Some 335 died riding the rails.

NEW DEAL MEASURES

The New Deal had to aid the young or the fabric of society would deteriorate. Its Civilian Conservation Corps sought to employ young people from eighteen to twenty-five in forestry. In nine years it hired 2,000,000 youths to work on projects connected with protection of the environment.

(50)

Top, left: CCC camps offered young men a vigorous, useful life at low pay. Top, right: some camps offered skilled farm labor recruits. Blacks were kept in segregated camps. Bottom, right: CCC camp food was nourishing, but not tasty; still, it was better than starving.

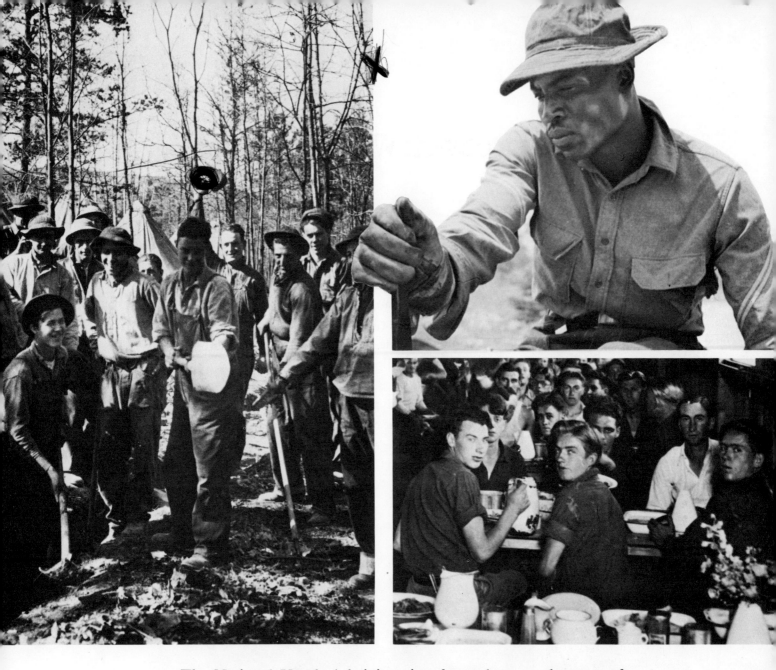

The National Youth Administration focused on employment of youth from relief families. It also provided college or high school students with part- or full-time jobs. Times were hard for those trying to stay in school. Some students sang:

But in pursuit of knowledge
We are starving by degrees.

Like other New Deal laws, although the CCC and the NYA employed millions, other millions were still without jobs. Spirits picked up, but the grim face of hard times remained.

The Depression Weather

THE FLOODS

Each week film audiences sat through another newsreel showing yet another flood rampaging through a city or town. They watched beds and rag dolls float away, Red Cross volunteers feed survivors, and churning waters cascade through shopping areas.

During the thirties these American rivers vaulted their banks: the Mississippi, Ohio, Potomac, Tennessee, Delaware, Connecticut, Missouri, Susquehanna, Columbia, Allegheny, and Merrimack. The 1937 Ohio flood was the worst in U.S. history, washing away 500,000 homes. In this decade floods and windstorms took 3,678 lives, and made the Great Depression more depressing.

DUST STORMS

As if the economic crisis was not enough, farmers had to contend with worse. Their farms blew away.

The dry, parched season of 1930 turned into dust storms in 1931 and 1932. Then came 1933. In the ninth month of the New Deal, nature dealt its harshest hand. On Armistice Day morning farms in South Dakota spun away. By noon the sky was dark. The next day's sun rose on sand dunes not dirt. Sheds and tractors were buried in sand. The searing sands wound their way to Texas, darkened part of Chicago, and were seen as far east as Albany, New York.

In 1934 and 1935 howling windstorms continued. Cattle and sheep died of thirst or were buried alive in swirling sands. Entire towns were coated with fine dust. Mothers and children packed keyholes and windows with oiled cloth and gummed paper. They stayed inside and prayed. Water and food tasted gritty.

(53)

Opposite, left: Harry Hopkins inspected WPA efforts to halt a rampaging flood in 1936. Opposite, right: floods such as this one in Hancock, Maryland, left thousands homeless. Above: Farmer and Son in a Dust Storm *is the title of this Oklahoma photo.*

The Sharecropper Tragedy

AMERICA'S NO. 1 PROBLEM

A New Deal report found the South to be the nation's #1 economic problem. More people tried to live on less valuable land at lower wages than anywhere else. Cotton, the South's main crop, depleted the soil. It used the cheapest workers and suffered the biggest market fluctuations.

The sharecropper and his family were America's forgotten people. Husband and wife worked for a landowner who controlled their lives and paid them with a portion of their crop. They were often cheated, especially if they were black.

When the AAA paid landowners to reduce their crops and planting, sharecroppers were fired by the thousands. They were driven from the homes provided for them. By winter 1935 dispossessed blacks and whites crowded the roads of rural Arkansas, victims of the AAA plan.

(55)

Opposite: a Dameron, Maryland, home with eleven children
that received aid from the Farm Security Administration.
Above: the problems of underpaid and oppressed
agricultural workers in the South concerned the New Deal.

THE FARM SECURITY ADMINISTRATION (FSA)

To help sharecroppers and other homeless urban and rural people find loans and homes, FDR established the FSA. He appointed Rexford G. Tugwell of his Brain Trust to run it. Tugwell built new communities for the homeless and provided families with loans.

A unique aspect of the plan was his hiring of a team of top photographers. Ben Shahn, Gordon Parks, Dorothea Lange, and Arthur Rothstein were sent out with cameras to record the story of how Americans lived during hard times. Many of their photographs appear in this book.

SHARECROPPERS UNITE FOR ACTION

In Arkansas black and white sharecroppers formed the Southern Tenant Farmers Union. When they tried to improve their conditions, they were arrested, beaten, and tortured. Yet their union held on.

(57)

Opposite: cotton pickers in Pulaski, Arkansas, in 1935,
one of the regions hardest hit by A A A cutbacks in
crop production. Above: in 1936 these agricultural
workers decided to unite in a union across racial lines.

The Power of the Radical Right

CONSERVATIVE OPPOSITION TO FDR MOUNTS

America had no tradition to prepare it for the New Deal. No U.S. government had ever spent money to feed the poor, promote social welfare, or hire the unemployed. Common enough today, these actions were viewed then as suspicious steps toward socialism or government control of daily life.

Once business began to recover, its leaders led the attack on FDR's New Deal. Some feared his aid to unions, the destitute, and the unemployed, and a few openly admired Hitler's crushing of unions and radicals. In the United States, Governor Huey Long and Father Charles Coughlin tried to unite the conservative distrust of FDR behind their own drive for power.

HUEY LONG

Born into a poor backwoods Louisiana family, Huey Long learned how to climb the ladder of success. He worked his way through college, became a lawyer and then governor of Louisiana. He said he wanted to "make every man a king" and jokingly called himself "the Kingfish."

As governor, Long lowered taxes on the poor and raised them on the wealthy. He became popular by building schools, hospitals, and roads and by providing pupils with free textbooks and bus rides to school. He also made a fortune while doing this.

The Kingfish's homey manner masked an iron will and relentless ambition. His foes found their homes bombed, their lives threatened. Armed bodyguards shielded the Kingfish whenever he went out. His legislature passed forty-four bills in twenty-two minutes, a record for a democracy. But few believed that Louisiana under Governor Long was a democracy. He once entered New Orleans leading the National Guard and threatening his enemies with "I'll dynamite them out of my path!"

Opposite: Governor Herbert Lehman, Eleanor Roosevelt, and Mayor Fiorello La Guardia of New York City were special targets of the radical right in the 1936 elections. Above: "Kingfish" Huey Long first supported FDR, then became a bitter foe.

Above: to escape the economic crisis, many took refuge in the church. Father Divine built a huge empire for black and white followers. Opposite: radio priest Father Charles Coughlin was heard by millions each week.

One rainy night in 1935 as the Kingfish left the Capitol, a figure stepped out of the shadows and fired a pistol at him. As Long lay dying, his guards riddled the assassin with machine-gun fire. Long might have run for President in 1936, but now he was dead. His followers sang mournfully:

Oh, they say he was a crook
But he gave us free school book
Tell me why is it that they killed Huey Long?

FATHER CHARLES COUGHLIN, THE RADIO PRIEST

From Detroit, Father Charles Coughlin beamed his weekly radio broadcast to millions across the country. Each week he received more mail than the President and $20,000 in contributions. His message was one of hate.

He denounced FDR and his "Jew Deal" and warned that Jews, foreigners, and unions were responsible for the nation's evils. He urged his followers to form rifle clubs and attack Jews on the streets of New York City; he suggested FDR's elimination "by use of bullets."

The radio priest edged toward fascism, Hitler, and a desire to run the government. In 1936 he and the Long followers launched their greatest effort to win the government.

(61)

The Election of 1936

THE ANTI-FDR FORCES MOBILIZE

The Republicans chose Governor Alf Landon of Kansas as their candidate for President and sang:

> *Oh, Alf Landon!*
> *He's the man for me!*
> *'Cause he comes from Prairie Kansas*
> *His country for to free!*

The *Literary Digest* predicted Landon would sweep to victory, and the Republicans were jubilant.

Dr. Townsend, Father Coughlin, and Gerald L. K. Smith, heir to the Huey Long forces, united behind the Union Party and its candidate, Congressman William Lemke. They talked openly of seizing the government. Smith shouted, "I'll teach them [voters] how to hate," and Coughlin announced, "I take the road of fascism."

Landon conducted a poor campaign also. He began by saying, "Wherever I have gone in this country, I have found Americans." He ended by claiming FDR was influenced by Communists and Jews.

THE FDR LANDSLIDE

The President campaigned against "economic royalists" and told a cheering audience, "I welcome their hate."

On election day FDR carried every state except Maine and Vermont. He joked, "I knew I should have campaigned in Maine and Vermont." But it was no joke that 5,000,000 Republicans had voted for the New Deal, that three-quarters of the House and Senate were Democrats. Lemke drew less than 1,000,000 votes, while FDR received 28,000,000.

Roosevelt had a clear mandate to continue his plans. He was at the height of his popularity. In time, forty-one songs would be written about him. But minefields lay ahead for his New Deal.

Top: the FDR family was an effective campaign image, shown here in 1936 before the White House. Center, left: Governor Alfred Landon of Kansas campaigns in New York City. Center, right: FDR, campaigning in the field, went on to win four terms as President. Bottom: increasingly, FDR drew votes of the disaffected from the radical right and left.

The New Deal Crests in 1937

FDR'S SECOND TERM

President Roosevelt began his new term with more popular support than ever before. Much more needed to be done. "I see one-third of a nation ill-housed, ill-clad, ill-nourished," FDR said at his Inauguration. Yet the President headed toward trouble, and some of his own making.

THE 1937 DEPRESSION

In the summer of 1937 stock prices began to tumble again. Steel production fell to a fifth of capacity. Within a year, 2,000,000 people had lost their jobs. Fear again stalked the land. This Depression could not be blamed on Hoover or the Republicans.

This time FDR was to blame. He never wanted to spend large amounts of government money. He spent too little, and unemployment again soared. The New Deal rushed to increase WPA funds and aid to the economy.

Above: flush with his huge victory over Landon and the Republicans, FDR and Vice President Henry Wallace prepared to advance his New Deal. Opposite, top: breadlines again appeared, like this one in Chicago. Opposite, bottom: one-third of a nation was still without adequate food, clothing, and shelter.

THE SUPREME COURT BATTLE

FDR had become increasingly angry with the U.S. Supreme Court. It had nullified his AAA and NRA and appeared poised to strike down other New Deal laws. FDR charged that the High Court was "back in the horse-and-buggy days." But he planned more than denunciations.

He proposed that Congress pass a law enlarging the Supreme Court. He wanted to appoint his own Justices. Both enemies and supporters were revolted at this idea of altering the Court because FDR disagreed with its decisions. His plan never came to a vote in Congress.

It turned out to be unnecessary. In the next four years, with deaths and retirements, FDR appointed seven Justices. And the Supreme Court began to approve New Deal laws.

But with the "Roosevelt Depression" and his efforts to control the Supreme Court, FDR lost friends and support in Congress. The New Deal was on its way out. In the following years it would pass few measures.

(66)

Left: the "Roosevelt Depression" threw many out of work again and brought protestors to Washington.
Right: a worried FDR prepared to address the nation by radio on his plan to enlarge the Supreme Court.

Unions Organize Industrially

SPLIT IN THE AMERICAN FEDERATION OF LABOR

At the beginning of the Great Depression only one in nineteen workers was a union member. The conservative AFL, under William Green, dominated the field, and half of its members had slipped away in the twenties. It accepted only skilled craftsmen, rejected women, minorities, and the unskilled millions who worked in mass production industries.

At the 1935 AFL convention John L. Lewis, president of the United Mine Workers (UMW), challenged the organization to unionize steel, rubber, car, farm machinery, and textile workers. When the AFL refused, Lewis withdrew his UMW and began forming what would become the Congress of Industrial Organizations (CIO). Lewis sent out his organizers shouting, "The President wants you to join!"

Lewis capitalized on FDR's encouragement to unions and new laws protecting their right of collective bargaining.

(67)

Left: unemployment demonstrations reflected the lack of jobs. Right: John L. Lewis (right) and clothing workers' president, Sidney Hillman, organized the Congress of Industrial Organizations to challenge the conservative AFL.

THE CIO COLLIDES WITH EMPLOYERS

Lewis knew his task would not be easy. Union organizers lived in fear of their lives. Men and women worked under the guns of company guards in many plants and mines. To counter the CIO drive, corporations moved on two fronts. By 1935 they had organized 2,500,000 workers in their own "company unions." In 1936 alone they spent some $80,000,000 on spies and detectives.

The CIO plunged ahead, braving the spies and challenging the company unions. In five years the CIO unionized 3,000,000 men and women, black and white, skilled and unskilled. Even the AFL doubled its membership.

(69)

Opposite: conflict marked the house of labor—between the AFL and CIO and on the industrial firing line. Above: women strikers were not uncommon during the hard times.

The Unions' Two Greatest Battles

THE SIT-DOWN STRIKES

The CIO was hardly a year old when it developed a dramatic technique for winning strikes without violence. Its car workers struck in Michigan to win union recognition. Instead of leaving the plant and picketing, they remained in the factories and brought in food. Explained one worker: "Shut off the machinery and pack your tail right there. Yes, sir. We got our own patrol to protect company property . . . commissary and sanitation committees . . . no smoking allowed and no drinking."

The United Auto Workers under Walter Reuther won recognition for the union. The sit-down spread to the textile, oil-refining, and shipbuilding industries. Some 500,000 men and women staged sit-down strikes.

There was no violence, as employers dared not bring strikebreakers into the plants for fear fighting would damage their machinery. But the Supreme Court finally outlawed sit-down strikes.

THE MEMORIAL DAY MASSACRE

Corporations rarely surrendered easily to the new unions. The steel industry was the most resistant and successful in confronting unions.

On Memorial Day 1937 steelworkers marched from a picnic to the Republic Steel plant near Chicago to present their petition for a union. As the front line of their long march neared the company gates, they were met by police and guards. Suddenly the police opened fire on the front lines and charged, swinging their clubs.

The marchers fled, leaving ten dead and eighty-four wounded. Pathé News recorded the event on film, but never showed it publicly. Steel remained unorganized.

(71)

Opposite, left: sit-down strikers at a Flint, Michigan, auto plant read the papers. Opposite, center: sit-downers leaving a plant after a victory. Opposite, right: Woolworth saleswomen stage their own sit-down strike. Above: the Memorial Day Massacre as recorded by Pathé News.

Minorities Drive for Justice

THE HARDEST HIT

"The Depression brought everybody down a peg or two," wrote poet Langston Hughes, but nonwhites "had few pegs to fall." Traditionally they were the last hired and the first fired. The Depression did not change that.

In Chicago the 4 percent black population made up 16 percent of the unemployed and in Houston the black 25 percent were half the jobless. To preserve jobs for whites and cut back on relief rolls, Mexican-Americans were illegally deported. In Los Angeles alone, in 1932, 11,000 Mexican-Americans were seized and sent to Mexico.

But for the white majority, the Depression provided a new interracial experience. Being jobless and destitute for the first time, they lined up with blacks at breadlines, soup kitchens, and for government aid. "We're in the same boat, brother" went a popular tune.

RESISTANCE MOUNTS

The Depression sparked strikes and protest by nonwhites. In California Chicanos and Filipinos organized their own unions and conducted agricultural strikes.

When nine black youths were arrested in Alabama in 1932 and railroaded to jail on the false charge of raping two white women (one of whom admitted in open court that it was a lie), a worldwide protest campaign began. The Scottsboro Boys were saved from the death penalty, but all served long prison terms before winning release or escaping. Not until 1976 did the last man win a pardon.

In 1939 contralto Marian Anderson was denied the right to sing at Constitution Hall by the Daughters of the American Revolution. Led by Harold Ickes, Secretary of the Interior, and Eleanor Roosevelt, protesters arranged an open concert at the Lincoln Memorial. Ms. Anderson sang before 75,000 Americans.

Top, left: the mothers of the Scottsboro defendants in a May Day parade in New York. Top, right: Marian Anderson sings at the Lincoln Memorial. Center, left: Langston Hughes, poet laureate of the black ghettoes. Center, right: Chicago pickets protest working conditions and discrimination. Bottom: FDR tried to be President of "all the people."

The New Deal and Minorities

DISCRIMINATION LIVES ON

FDR, as was true of his predecessors, never dared challenge discrimination or even lynchings. More than a hundred black people were lynched in the thirties, but FDR refused to speak out. "If I come out for the anti-lynching bill now," he told blacks, "[southern congressmen] will block every bill I ask Congress to pass to keep America from collapsing. I just can't take that risk."

New Deal agencies allowed discrimination to continue. Low-cost housing for whites and blacks was segregated. The NRA, TVA, and WPA paid whites at higher rates than blacks. CCC camps were segregated, as was the armed forces. The brutal chain gangs and prison camps of the South were never condemned by the President.

*Opposite: this stark photo of a Georgia
prison camp in 1941 tells its own story about
progress in racial relations in the South. Above:
a 1936 photoessay by Dorothea Lange portrays
race relations in Clarksdale, Mississippi.*

FDR AND MINORITIES

However, in FDR and particularly in Eleanor Roosevelt, minorities in America felt they had a champion. President Roosevelt spoke for "the forgotten man" and said the lowly should benefit from government legislation. He told the Daughters of the American Revolution: "Remember, remember always that all of us, and you and I especially, are descended from immigrants and revolutionists."

To advise on racial matters, FDR became the first President to appoint a "Black Cabinet." Ralph Bunche, Robert Weaver, and Mary McCleod Bethune served New Deal agencies.

At election time blacks and ethnic minorities swung their allegiance to the Democrats and FDR. In large cities this ethnic and black vote became crucial to New Deal victories at the polls.

(76)

Left: during the hard times, minorities spoke out as never before in the general protests. This delegation seeks admission to the White House. Right: Robert Weaver, who later became the first black cabinet member under President Johnson, first held a Washington job during the New Deal.

Women on the March

MYTH AND REALITY

To judge from Hollywood films, women wanted only to stay at home, rear children, and please their husbands. But even when the emphasis was on "getting *men* back to work," 500,000 women entered the work force. For women who were heads of families working was a necessity, and for other families it often meant a bit more than enough to eat.

Three outstanding women of the 1930s were Eleanor Roosevelt, Frances Perkins, and Mary McCleod Bethune.

ELEANOR ROOSEVELT

More than simply FDR's wife, Eleanor Roosevelt was an outspoken champion of human rights. Her weekly radio broadcasts, her newspaper columns, and her fifteen books made her one of the world's most admired citizens.

Left: women spoke out as never before during the New Deal era.
Center: Eleanor Roosevelt
Above, right: Mary McCleod Bethune
Below, right: Frances Perkins with William Green, president of the AFL.

Eleanor dared to speak out on controversial issues, associated with black causes and friends, and denounced injustice wherever she found it. When she asked FDR if her stands were hurting his career, he reportedly replied, "Lady, it's a free country!"

Year after year American women voted her the most admired woman in the land. On FDR's death, Eleanor was appointed to represent the United States at the United Nations. From 1946 to 1953 she served as chairwoman of the U.N. Commission on Human Rights.

FRANCES PERKINS

As Secretary of Labor, Frances Perkins served during one of the most tumultuous decades. She found herself more on the side of unions than FDR, and did not hesitate to state her views.

During a party she listened to Harry Hopkins explain his WPA idea. She introduced Hopkins to FDR, and WPA was born and a most vital member of the Brain Trust had been found.

Frances Perkins also had the distinction of presiding over the Cabinet committee that drew up the Social Security plan. As long as FDR lived, Frances Perkins was Secretary of Labor.

MARY McCLEOD BETHUNE

One of seventeen children born to ex-slave parents on a cotton plantation in South Carolina, Ms. Bethune became an educator and champion for black America. With six students and $1.50 she began what became Bethune-Cookman College in Florida.

FDR appointed Ms. Bethune to the National Youth Administration and she became a leading member of the "Black Cabinet" that advised FDR on racial matters. With Eleanor, she besieged the President with demands to halt discrimination and save black victims of injustice.

"You always come asking help for others—never for yourself," FDR told her, adding, "I'm always glad to see you."

Left: the crooning hero of the decade, until Bing Crosby came around, was Rudy Vallee, star of radio and movies. Right: glamour came first in Hollywood. Carole Lombard is made up before the cameras roll.

Popular Culture Grows

THE FILM DECADE

Once a week half the U.S. population went to the films. They thrilled to Hollywood stars, to cowboys fighting Indians, and to King Kong. Fifty gangster films were produced each year. But most popular were the films that diverted people from the hard times. Chorus lines of jewel-bedecked women danced down marble staircases, and poor girls found and married rich men.

The truth rarely shone from the silver screen. The hit of the decade was *Gone With the Wind*. It pictured a South during slavery of contented blacks and kind whites. In other films minorities rarely appeared, or if they did, they were portrayed as childlike, vicious, stupid, or sinister. Women were pretty but dumb, and dependent upon men.

RADIO

Everyone listened to the radio, and networks sent the same broadcasts from New York to California. Young and old laughed at Bob Hope's jokes, enjoyed Bing Crosby's songs, and thrilled to the gangster programs. "Gangbusters" opened with roaring machine guns. "The Shadow" moved invisibly against crime. Buck Rogers fought crooks in the future world of the twenty-first century. "The Lone Ranger" battled outlaws in the Old West.

Opposite, top: Shirley Temple delighted audiences and dances here with Bill Robinson. Opposite, center: Clark Gable and Myrna Loy were among the stars of the Depression years in Hollywood. Opposite, bottom, left: tough man James Cagney starred in gangster and Western films, and in one film pushed a grapefruit in the face of a woman. Opposite, bottom, right: Bob Hope and Bing Crosby clown in one of their many "road pictures." Above: the antics of the wealthy fascinated moviegoers during hard times.

(81)

THE COMICS

In 1934, with *Famous Funnies,* comic books made their appearance in America. Millions of young and old bought *Superman, Batman and Robin,* and *Captain Marvel.*

In the classrooms of America a new teacher order was heard: "Please put that comic book away!"

SWING THAT MUSIC

The Jazz Age of the twenties was followed by the Swing Decade of the thirties. Benny Goodman, "the King of Swing," introduced young and old to the catchy tunes of the day. Dancers swirled to the jitterbug as huge bands played on.

Records ran at 78 rpm and sold for 35 to 50 cents. The leading singer was Bing Crosby, but a new young man named Frank Sinatra was slowly working his way up.

Some tried to forget the bad times by singing "Life is just a bowl of cherries." But when President Herbert Hoover asked singer Rudy Vallee to chose a tune that would make people forget the Depression, he sang instead:

> *Once I built a railroad, made it run*
> *Made it race against time.*
> *Once I built a railroad, now it's done.*
> *Brother, can you spare a dime?*

BASEBALL IS KING

The national pastime was baseball. In this decade the New York Yankees, with Babe Ruth, Lou Gehrig, and later Joe DiMaggio, won pennants and the World Series fairly regularly. Fans who could not afford the cheap seats listened to games on the radio.

The national pastime was lily-white. No black player was allowed to don a Big League uniform until after World War II.

Top: popular cowboy movies distorted history. Here Indians are played by whites, and black scout Jim Beckwourth is portrayed by white actor Jack Oakie (left). Bottom, right: the Yankees one-two punch was Lou Gehrig and Babe Ruth. Bottom, left: King of Swing Benny Goodman plays his clarinet, and Johnny Weissmuller, star of the Tarzan movies, screeches a Tarzan yell.

A Violent Decade

CITIZEN VIOLENCE

Driven by desperation, citizens and sometimes police took matters into their own hands. Employers commonly hired "guards" to assault union leaders, and southern prison camps and chain gangs were infamous. Student and worker strikes were often violent. In 1934 police fired on strikers in Ohio and Wisconsin, and longshoremen striking 2,000 miles (3220 km.) of Pacific coast clashed with police.

In this atmosphere certain crimes became "acceptable."

RISE IN CRIME

"The criminal in America is on the march," announced J. Edgar Hoover, whose FBI kept busy chasing gangsters. Those who robbed banks sometimes found themselves admired. People recalled that banks had foreclosed on hard-pressed farmers and shut down without returning the life savings of poor people. So bank robbers were often called modern Robin Hoods.

Most were plain hoods. Yet their names made headlines: Baby Face Nelson, Machine Gun Kelly, Bonnie and Clyde. The FBI engaged in machine-gun duels with crooks, and such films as *G-Men* glorified their actions.

Public Enemy No. 1 was John Dillinger. His bloody spree included at least ten murders, four bank stickups, and three jailbreaks. Despite this vicious record, many people admired him for his war against the establishment. One night, as he left a cops-and-robbers film, Dillinger was brought down by a hail of FBI bullets.

Opposite, left: a scene before the Congress on December 1, 1930. Opposite, right: during a May Day march these men depicted the horrors of southern chain gangs. Above, left: violence often accompanied demonstrations during the hard times. Police battle protestors at Battery Park, New York. Above, center: Public Enemy #1, John Dillinger. Above, right: these officers guarded Dillinger in jail. He escaped anyway.

The First Protest Decade

INSTANT PROTEST

More than any previous time in history, the thirties saw an explosion of protest organizations, demonstrations, and petitions. Unemployment Councils, Workers' Alliances, anti-war groups, and advocates of racial equality marched, shouted, and circulated pamphlets and petitions.

May Day parades in New York brought out thousands who marched to Union Square and listened and cheered Communist speakers.

Radicals and friends helped dispossessed city families move back into their tenements. Blacks picketed against discrimination and joined with whites to protest lynchings and segregation in the South.

In Harlem, young Adam Clayton Powell, Jr., led "Don't Buy Where You Can't Work" campaigns. The black ghetto's main shopping area on 125th Street was white-owned and operated. Powell's campaign, and a four-day riot in 1935, finally forced each store to hire at least one black salesperson.

THE RISE AND FALL OF RADICALISM

FDR's own experimentalism stimulated an interest in socialism. Many intellectuals found socialism or communism attractive, and radicals sought to organize citizens for a socialist revolution. Communists attached themselves to many protests and sought to transform them into a movement toward socialism.

*Opposite, left: women played a prominent part
in protests of aggression abroad. Opposite, right:
blacks demonstrated against discrimination.
Above, left: Columbia University students
struck against the expulsion of a young man.
Above, right: protests, such as this Pittsburgh
Communist march, highlighted the 1930s.*

(87)

New York City's Flamboyant Mayor La Guardia

1933

When Fiorello La Guardia was elected mayor of New York in 1933 the largest community in the world had lost heart. There were 1,000,000 jobless men and women and eighty-two breadlines throughout the five boroughs of the city. One-fifth of the schoolchildren suffered from malnutrition. The unemployed fought police. Hoovervilles sprouted in Central Park and stretched along Riverside Drive from 72nd Street to 110th Street.

The pint-sized, peppery little man named La Guardia seemed made for the job. Born to Italian and Jewish parents, he could speak to New Yorkers in their own languages. He had been a Socialist, a Republican, and a New Dealer—and radical ideas did not upset him. He boasted he could defeat his political foes "running on a laundry ticket." He probably could have.

"WHO'S AFRAID OF THE BIG BAD WOLF?"

La Guardia's five-foot-two frame bounced around the city like a rubber ball. He led police raids, arrived at fires in an outsize Fire Chief hat, and once read the comics over the radio to children during a newspaper strike. He had a flair for publicity and a commitment to reform.

Fearful of no one, La Guardia's theme song was "Who's Afraid of the Big Bad Wolf?" He ordered the arrest of top gangsters, took the side of striking workers, and hired minority members in his administration. He built parks in slum areas.

Despite his clowning and his mistakes, New Yorkers knew La Guardia was around when they needed him. After World War II he was put in charge of relief for the United Nations. Now he cared for the world.

Top, left: Mayor La Guardia during a truck strike in New York City. Top, right: His Honor throws out the first ball of the new baseball season. Bottom, left: La Guardia and labor leader John L. Lewis. Bottom, right: La Guardia leads the orchestra in Central Park on Mother's Day.

The Lengthening Shadow of War

RISE OF FASCISM

About thirty days separated FDR's first Inauguration and Hitler's appointment as Chancellor of Germany. Yet an ocean of difference separated their approaches to the problems of unemployment and economic collapse. Where the New Deal provided jobs and relief, Hitler gave Germany military power and racial hatred. Dictatorships in Italy and Japan also armed and prepared for war.

Hostilities began in 1931 when Japan attacked Manchuria. Soon Germany absorbed Austria and Czechoslovakia and prepared to attack Poland. Italy invaded Ethiopia and Japan attacked China. By 1936 Italy and Germany had forged an alliance that made a new war inevitable. Unable to halt aggression, the League of Nations was falling apart.

Americans ignored the war danger and resented FDR for pushing it into their consciousness. But America was unprepared for war. Half the tanks in the 1937 Inaugural parade broke down in front of the President. FDR increased the nation's military power and in 1940 introduced the first peacetime draft in U.S. history.

THE FASCIST DANGER
INTRUDES ON AMERICA

Increasingly, Americans became aware of the Nazi persecution of minorities and Germany's aggressive tactics. U.S. citizens objected to participation in the 1936 Olympic Games in Germany, and in the port of New York some stormed a Nazi ship and tore down its flag.

In 1936 when German Max Schmeling knocked out Joe Louis, Detroit's Brown Bomber, the Nazis proclaimed this proof of "the superiority of the German Aryan race." In 1938 an angry Joe Louis entered Madison Square Garden before 80,000 fans to face Schmeling again. Within two minutes of the first round the Nazi had been knocked out, and Joe Louis was again world champion heavyweight king.

Americans remained deeply divided over the war danger. The America First Committee demanded U.S. isolationism and strict neutrality. When General Franco, with Nazi and Fascist aid, overthrew the Republican government of Spain, the U.S. remained neutral. However, an Abraham Lincoln Brigade of American volunteers fought against the Franco forces.

Opposite, left: Max Schmeling and Joe Louis weigh in for the world heavyweight title bout in 1938. In less than three minutes of the first round, Schmeling was knocked out. Opposite, right: Albert Einstein (right) was one of the famous scientists who fled fascism to settle in America. Above: Nazi forces were on the march throughout Europe.

(91)

President Roosevelt Becomes "Dr. Win the War"

WORLD WAR II BEGINS

In September 1939 Adolf Hitler ordered his Stuka bombers and Panzer divisions into Poland. World War II had begun. Britain and France declared war on Germany and Italy. War matériel orders began flowing into the United States.

Unemployment all but vanished as industries hummed and young Americans entered the armed forces.

Public attention was now riveted on the fast-moving events in Europe. People and the Congress, reported Harry Hopkins, were "bored with the poor, the unemployed and the insecure." America's allies seemed on the brink of defeat.

PEARL HARBOR

At about ten minutes to eight on the Sunday morning of December 7, 1941, Japanese planes swooped out of the sky over Pearl Harbor and virtually destroyed the American Pacific Fleet. Planes were smashed on the ground. Ships were sunk at anchor. America had been caught napping.

The next day FDR asked Congress for a Declaration of War and the United States entered World War II. The armed forces swelled and the nation moved toward a war footing. "Dr. New Deal has been replaced by Dr. Win the War," the President announced. The hard times were all but forgotten as Americans pitched in to defeat the grave threat to democracy and world peace.

The Great Depression was finally over. But FDR and the New Deal had not defeated the hard times. They had cared, spent, and hired, but not spent or done enough. Until the United States entered the war, millions were still without work, and some Americans lived close to starvation. For all its efforts, the New Deal had not solved the Depression. The war had done that.

Top, left: only the war lifted America out of the Depression, for in 1939 this crowd of women lined up for twelve New York City jobs paying $960 a year. Top, right: FDR becomes Dr. Win the War. Watching U.S. armored units in Casablanca in 1943. Center, left: Hollywood also rushed off to war. Center, right: by the time of the attack on Pearl Harbor, the Hoovervilles had been torn down. Bottom: lettuce workers in 1939, still underemployed and underpaid.

Bibliography

Frederick Lewis Allen, *Since Yesterday* (New York, Harper and Row, 1939).

Erskine Caldwell and Margaret Bourke-White, *You Have Seen Their Faces* (New York, Modern Age Books, 1939).

Robert Goldston, *The Great Depression* (Greenwich, Conn., Fawcett Publications, 1968).

James D. Horan, *The Desperate Years* (New York, Bonanza Books, 1962).

William Loren Katz, *Eyewitness: The Negro in American History* (New York, Pitman, 1974).

———. *Years of Strife, 1929–1956* (New York, Franklin Watts, 1975).

Dorothea Lange and Paul Schuster Taylor, *An American Exodus* (New Haven, Conn., Yale University Press, 1969).

William E. Leuchtenburg, *Franklin D. Roosevelt and the New Deal* (New York, Harper Torchbooks, 1963).

William Manchester, *The Glory and the Dream* (New York, Bantam, 1974).

Alfred B. Rollins, Jr., *Franklin D. Roosevelt and the Age of Action* (New York, Dell, 1960).

David A. Shannon, ed., *The Great Depression* (Englewood Cliffs, N.J., Prentice-Hall, 1960).

Roy Emerson Stryker and Nancy Wood, *In This Proud Land* (Boston, Mass., New York Graphic Society, 1973).

Studs Terkel, *Hard Times* (New York, Random House, 1970).

Ben D. Zevin, ed., *Nothing to Fear* (New York, Popular Library, 1961).

Index